Opening The Black Ovule Gate

poems by

Lisa Rhodes-Ryabchich

Finishing Line Press
Georgetown, Kentucky

Opening The Black Ovule Gate

Copyright © 2018 by Lisa Rhodes-Ryabchich
ISBN 978-1-63534-411-0 First Edition
All rights reserved under International and Pan-American Copyright Conventions.
No part of this book may be reproduced in any manner whatsoever without written permission from the publisher, except in the case of brief quotations embodied in critical articles and reviews.

Acknowledgements:

I want to graciously thank my mother Rosemarie Rhodes and father Joel Rhodes and sister Leslie Ann Rhodes for their support in writing this manuscript and providing details and information that made this story compelling. Special thanks to Aunt Shirley for her knowledge and Aunt Desiree for a photograph of my Aunt Betty all which helped nurture these poems.

Grateful thanks to the writers and staff at Poets Corner in New Rochelle, N.Y. for their support and encouragement and where these poems were first performed, Dan Masterson for his editing and advice, Kevin Pilkington, Suzanne Cleary, Claudine Nash, Michael Collins, Greg Roman, Cornelius Eady, Douglas Brown, Jacqueline Jones Lamon, Nicole Sealey, Cave Canem, John Snypes, Nicole Davis Coleman, Richie Ramphal, Jennifer Chadee, Lisa Jewell, Yusef Komunyakaa, Martha Rhodes, Myronn Hardy, Gregory Pardlo, Michael Affa Weaver, Francine J Harris, Evie Shockley, Jean Valentine, Tracy K Smith, Christopher Citro, Arthur Weinstein and Martha's Vineyard Creative Writing Center, Rockland Poets, Jeffrey McDaniel for his encouragement and support, Susan Guma, Thomas Lux for believing in my talents, Sarah Lawrence College where these poems were first written and originated over a 2016 summer writing seminar, and Matt Rasmussen for his support and writing workshop.

Heartfelt thanks to the following journals and anthologies in which these poems or earlier versions first appeared:
Madness Muse Press Destigmatized Anthology: "The Cocoon."
The Moon Magazine: "The End."

Sincere thanks to Finishing Line Press for their belief in my poetic talents and for helping bring these poems to a larger audience.

Publisher: Leah Maines
Editor: Christen Kincaid
Cover Art: Fredrick Letzter
Author Photo: Glamour Shots
Cover Design: Elizabeth Maines McCleavy

Printed in the USA on acid-free paper.
Order online: www.finishinglinepress.com
        also available on amazon.com

Author inquiries and mail orders:
Finishing Line Press
P. O. Box 1626
Georgetown, Kentucky 40324
U. S. A.

Table of Contents

Auntie Betty's Suicide 1969 1

Before You Committed Suicide 2

Memory 3

Divorce Papers 4

Suicide Planning 5

The Murder 6

Auntie Betty's Manifesto 7

The End 9

The Cocoon 10

Elegy for Cousin Charles 12

Christmas 13

Details 17

The Wake 18

The Black Hole 19

Tragedy 20

Goodbye Cousin Charles and Auntie Betty 22

AUNTIE BETTY'S SUICIDE 1969

After you committed murder
of your [son:husband] you climbed into
your white ceramic tub, slashed your thin
wrists to tissue paper, turned on cold
water to the fill line and let your
10 pints of *Black/Portuguese* blood drip.

We all tried to patch up your unloved
veins with intellectual sutures
then downed self-hate pills to stop the pain—
blocked the soresun from shining in
our altered lives, then my mother
masqueraded in green tint sun
glasses for most of her natural life.

BEFORE YOU COMMITTED SUICIDE

I remember you grabbing the black steel
pan off of the greasy white stove,
then waving it at my mother like a hammer as
you screamed, "Your husband made a pass at me!"

My mother just looked at you right in
your eye and sadly said, "No, No!" Six-year-old
I was there watching you in that cramped
Bronx kitchen. The three of us only inches

apart. I didn't flinch or run to my
mother to protect her or try to
grab the pan out of your hand. You accused
my father of something terrible

and I can't imagine he would have
wanted you! You confused, and jealous—
a copycat. My mother was an RN
then you became one too. My mother

married a handsome man, then you married
one too. Why did you try to become her?
Why did you want everything she had?
Once you told my mother,

"If you ever commit suicide,
I'll take your children for you."
What a monster mother you turned out to be.
I am not like you nor will I ever be.

MEMORY

Your boyfriend did something very
terrible to my sister. I
did not know this then. My mother
later told you she was very
angry; I never knew this…Years
later my sister told her friend
about it: the reasons why she
never got married. I wondered
if this was true. She had no memory
when asked, only a church girl sits
on the couch, only some memory
exists after your death and my
mother's silent indifference
and refusal to contact you
then. I understand anger; I
understand shame. A child's frightened
eyes tiptoe through darkness. I've tried
to go back there walking through that
apartment as a child on
that day, and you're still sitting on
the radiator with your boyfriend
next to you staring me away.
*It's dark. I don't know why he is
in our apartment; he shouldn't
be here.* Were you so insecure
about yourself that you needed someone
to watch you? Why did you bring him
there? Was this what your life was reduced
to after the breakup—hanging out with your
boyfriend? You were much prettier than that.

DIVORCE PAPERS

I remember the day you burned
                                  your husband's clothes
                                      in the incinerator

after he left you…
He told my dad that was it… if you ever did that again
                                  he was through…

He was such a bastard as he shoved
the divorce papers down your throat—under your door

when you were sleeping   after he got what he wanted:
Your money & empathy   for his latent ways.

SUICIDE PLANNING

She milks her lone child. Did she kiss him goodnight
with red morning glory lipstick? Apply a rouge
color to his already Santa Claus rosy cheeks?

She loves her hunky husband, paying to send him
to finish his B.S. in Economics degree.
How much did she love him, when contemplating their

son's death? Did she decide after a jealous flir-
tation in the kitchen, after sex was washed from
the dinner plate? Or did she plan his heavenly
breathtaking after two weeks of unrequited angst:

A divorce paper quickly jammed under her door
and her younger sister's husband's friendly visits
to console her, and the stigmata of *Black crazy single mom.*

THE MURDER

[Inside his depraved mother's head] it's better this way—
she shows me her evil smile
as the Joker from *Batman*.

[Inside my cousin's head] he shows me tragedy—
      the confusing white hospital grade pillow imploding—
his mother's hands pushing down a plastic bag around his head
forcefully as steel pincers.

[Inside my head] his little boy/man body was being taken
until finally there was no struggle.

         *

Why could he not fight her rage?
Why did he have no strength?

Did she drug him before?
Did she sing him soft lullabies as to a newborn?

         *

Your father and his family went
to [your funeral]—
I can barely remember his depressed handsome
figure passing through the black crowds of adults.

He later blocked you out like an aborted fetus.
He remarried and told no one about you.
Your birth was *lobotomized*.

         *

When your prominent father died—I'm sorry,
there was no mention of your *name*.

AUNTIE BETTY'S MANIFESTO

What was it like for me?—
a black woman in 1969
being served divorce papers—
the stigma? the shame?—
and having an undiagnosed mental illness.

No treatment... just shunned—thrown away
like garbage—*a cast-off?*
Suicidal anyway.
Could one win? Could there have been
any hope? I remember

Francis Farmer—her life was ruined.
She was seen as a sad lady—
crazy and useless. Ice picks jabbed
into her eye; she was left
emotionally vacant.

I remember my mother's sister Suzie—
her boyfriend kidnapped their daughter
because Suzie had a *nervous breakdown*.
Her daughter was never found.
I didn't want to lose my son.

Could one win?
No, no, I don't think so.
Men were not kind and forgiving.
My experience and what I knew of the world—
and what was taught to me by my father.

My mother was often beaten
by my father.
She almost died many times.
For mother: Black and blue,
I watched you struggle…

How you made it through, *God only knows*.
Who was there to stop him? No man
or brother, no neighbors—
I was just desperate to find love
From a handsome man.

I never saw any love in my father.
Born on his birthday—
I'm an outcast, somehow stigmatized
by his blood, his illness—his niceness
towards *only me* and not my mother.
Oh God, how you have us all confused.

THE END

Why was I jealous…?
                         Competitive?
                         I was pretty.

To be driven by self-respect, tenacity, resilience…
Where was mine? I copied my sister; I wanted to be her.

She was my role model, my *surrogate* mother.
I was nice to my nieces; I really loved them.

Pushed over the edge… from a loveless relationship—
it happens. I was outraged. My paychecks paid his tuition.

Desperation made my self-esteem low…
                         Illness can be so strong.

I was *Full* of self-hate… the desire to die. I was so confused.
I felt used—I didn't want a divorce.

Revengeful, I took my seed with me.
End the family, I told myself—total self-rejection.

I felt *cast away* like a bad seed, rejected & dejected.
Feeling like a whore who was going to be screwed—

a *failure*, I was ashamed— embarrassed…
                         I felt unloved, disillusioned by a lie

that I was ever in a *loving* relationship.

THE COCOON

Thunder grumbles as the rain
lightly pitter-patters like little
feet running. My cousin at age three

was jumping up to go to birthday
parties grinning like a *Daschund*
puppy happily bouncing on

his father's knee. He was a *spitting
image* of him eating grape jam
out at grandma's house, and sitting at

her kitchen table next to me, facing
the window where the miniature
sunlight became a floodlight of

stars, circling like doves, as we spent
time together on a Saturday
morning, waiting for the world

to spin us to another planet or
to go on the hospital boat
or back in time to the Worlds Fair or to

FAO Schwartz or to the plane-
tarium or to *heaven* and back again.
Those few hours together were

like a lifetime of memories
bound by a kitchen frame like
we were the last people on the planet.

How I don't want that memory
to fade—to be discarded away
like we were never idealistic

Christmas presents to our parents,
still lovely in their velvet skins,
and their hearts all a-glitter like

butterflies breaking out of their cocoons.

ELEGY FOR COUSIN CHARLES
for Charles Jr.

You suffocated from callous hands,
loss of love and desperate to make yourself

unborn again, graceful, and free—
trying to reach beyond the stars to get

that tough love,
flying in the wind, bursting onto

my neighbor's brown lawn.
1000's of hugs, waste onto the trees

occluding your chance to breathe—
red, raw and itchy, bristling along

my leg's spine.
You smelled like summer after it rained.

Have you ever redeemed yourself
from a life sentence?

"You can pretend to be the breeze
lifting you off to heaven,"

said a familiar voice so sweetly.
Babies are not chattel for lost love—

they are angels.
I hear the sounds of horns

and lutes in a symphony
under the eye of the killer loose inside us all—

that's where the *novocaine* must be fermenting.
And the rhythmic strumming of my fingers gets me high.

They have miniature love letters glued to their arches.

CHRISTMAS

It's Christmas week. Kyla your 2nd cousin
has finished playing with all her new toys.

They lay spread out on the soft purple mat.
We have abandoned them after hours of fun,

tracking light from them, then squeezing
the textures of sensory balls, playing

the drums & piano. It has been a joy;
I am exhausted. I dump the toys in

a box packed by the television. Next,
I leave to tuck Kyla into her electric

bed, that she loves to go up & down
on like a cool ride at the amusement park.

Just this fun feeling of moving is a thrill
for Kyla as she giggles & smiles this huge

grin that infects you with all kinds of desires
for miracles, of *what-ifs & what will-bes.*

I leave her bedroom to explore the living room
again. That's when the music starts to play

from one of her toys. I try to ignore it
thinking it has a faulty wiring or something

but then it plays again as the other toys
start to play. I get this eerie feeling that

you are in the room, playing with Kyla's
toys. You are smiling & looking at

me with those brown eyes, that make you smile.
I know you want to cry too but you don't.

I want to reach out to you. I don't.
I just watch you. I wonder why you came back

to visit? Because it's Christmas?
So we're all supposed to be happy?

How can there be so much happiness?
I almost don't want to believe that. Happiness

is transient. Sometimes we are dead to our emotions
and feel numb like we are suffocating ourselves

with grief—we don't feel the air on our fingers.
We don't feel there is any oxygen. Our own

unhappiness has built a semi-private prison in which
we are to contain ourselves. The cold air can be

invigorating at times. Maybe it keeps us going?
When cool air tempers our bad nerves,

it acts as our clock in which we measure
how much we can handle. Will we leave

when it gets too unbearable or will we
just sit it out being strong & thankful

that we made it through one more Christmas
knowing we are not alone? We still have air—

we still have our memories; we still have
our senses shielding us from the hereafter.

DETAILS

Did she lay you down, in the bed, in the spot,
your father would fall asleep when next to her—

on top of the white embroidered bedspread—your
head slanted against a red satin pillow?

Or did she reach down into your toy filled crib, then
drown the moist whispers of your warm sweet dream

like a planet expunging its race to space?
Did she tell you before you were no longer

able to *breathe fire*, into the empty
cold apartment that you were going to meet

sweet Jesus?—that you were a sacrifice for
her *tiny* God? Did she whisper lullabies

in your ear? Did she tell you, I love you—but
I'm so *sorry*, I'm so *sorry*, I'm so *sorry*…?

THE WAKE

When you died they put you in
the same casket with your mother
nestled together. A red velvet
curtain wrapped around like a
halo. I hated that image
years later. I didn't know
who it benefited, your
mother or you? Would you have
had no anger, if you had
known? Would you have wanted
her love or been forgiving
& kind? And I guess you would
have been an angel. Why had
I thought otherwise? I don't
know. I guess it's *heathenistic*
nature to imagine other-
wise. A sane person could only
provide a healing to one
that had gone insane.

THE BLACK HOLE

The space is all black. The computer screen
exhales like rich black eyes oozing in onyx.

This is a beauty no one can enjoy.
It is aftermath, of years of absence

of not knowing you ever existed
or asking why not. It's wondering—why

your life was taken. How could it have been
prevented? Would you have survived otherwise

without your mother? Or if she were to
have been institutionalized? Would you

have been like Malcolm X? Or an orphan,
or—adopted? Would you have survived a

step-mom? Your dad remarried. Did you ask
yourself why didn't she just kill your dad—

and not you? You were your own person—not
your dad, not your mom, just you. What could have

been was not; she *stole* your life and trashed her
own afterward. But I still ask, what could

have been? Maybe you could have been saved
had there been drugs for depression that worked—

had there been no *stigma*—
had your father loved her…

TRAGEDY

Tragedy is our signature.
It sits on our tombstone.
It waits until snowfall.
It hides in our bones.
It fly's like an insect with larvae.
It can be contained.
It can be eradicated like weeds—
Pulled from the flower garden
Until it blooms no more!

GOODBYE COUSIN CHARLES AND AUNT BETTY

Goodbye, I hope you know
    I've missed you both.
Till we meet again.
    Adieu.

I've missed you both.
    Time escaped the black clouds.
Till we meet again.
    Au revoir.

Time escaped the black clouds.
    Black birds send love.
Till we meet again.
    Tchau.

Lisa Rhodes-Ryabchich was born in New York City and lived at Fifth Ave., on 108th St., Harlem in a Co-op apartment across from Central Park Conservatory Gardens before moving with her family in 1968 to Orangeburg, N.Y. in Rockland County. It was 1992, when she left the Army, after she had lived in Seville, Spain as an foreign exchange student in 1989 and traveled around Europe and Scandinavia, when she had only a vague notion that she wanted to be a writer but after finding some of her mother's poems hidden in a drawer, she convinced herself that she too must have great metaphoric talent and began to take Dan Masterson's and Suzanne Cleary's poetry workshops at Rockland Community College in Suffern, N.Y. After she mastered those classes, she attended Sarah Lawrence College's Summer Seminar for Writers in Bronxville, N.Y. for three summers then applied to their MFA program and after 2 rejections, she joined their MFA poetry-writing program and graduated in 1999. Her mentor was Tom Lux and he was a marvelous teacher and very kind and caring. She was an enthusiastic student who interviewed Maxine Kumin over the phone for the "Phoenix" school newspaper. She had admired Anne Sexton and so just talking with Maxine was exciting. After graduating, she published some poems, worked as a life insurance agent, cashier at Pathmark (the 10pm-2am shift), substitute teacher and finally as an poetry instructor at Westchester Community College, an English Adjunct at Ramapo College and Bergen Community College before falling in love and getting married to a Russian Air-force Veteran in 2003. Her marriage ended tragically after her child got sick and finding out that her husband was unfit for marriage and raising a special-needs child. Luckily, her ability to turn lemons into lemonade enabled her to stay strong and persevere. After taking a few workshops through Cave Canem in NYC, she realized it was her or nobody that was going to make-it. She began to write more seriously and resurrected her poems from the forgotten files and started editing. Her hard work paid off and her first chapbook "We Are beautiful Like Snowflakes" was accepted for publication by http://www.finishinglinepress.com. She was glorified!

Furthermore, she is a strong self-determined single-mom of a 14-year old 120-pound lovable child named Kyla. Kyla is her only daughter, born when she turned 40 years old. Her daughter has a disabling condition called quadriplegia, cerebral palsy, and epilepsy. She was her miracle child who survived Strep B Meningitis, which she contracted at 6 weeks of age after being born at 36 weeks. Her child has beaten the odds and survived a horrible illness. Her child is non-verbal but can use yes/no signs when prompted. She has a beautiful smile and a great spirit. Lisa has thanked God her child has receptive skills and understands what she says to her otherwise she would not feel that halo of love after complimenting her and get to see her pearly white teeth and dimples flash. Throughout her 14-year journey with her daughter she has written articles as well as numerous poems about her daughter's illnesses. Her poetry manuscript about her daughter's fight with Strep B Meningitis is entitled "The Fight To Live" and is presently seeking a publisher. Her daughter, Kyla has been a huge advocate and inspiration for her writing. Her daughter's little face lights up when she reads her the poems and she feels urged on to write after seeing her daughter's gleeful enthusiasm. She knows her daughter wants her to be successful because she feels her daughter takes pride in her many accomplishments because after all her daughter has helped to implement them.

Additionally, Lisa presently teaches English World Literature at The University of the People, an online free tuition school and poetry at Westchester Community College. She teaches a free memoir, fiction, poetry writing class at Piermont Library and teaches classes elsewhere. She performs her poetry throughout the United States. Her poetry blog is: http://www.lisarhodesryabchichpoetryblog.wordpress.com which lists all her poetry readings. She also has a B.A. in Communications from St. Thomas Aquinas College in Sparkill, N.Y., a Computer Science Certificate in Business Applications from SUNY Purchase in Purchase, N.Y., a B.S. in Journalism from Mercy College in Dobbs Ferry, N.Y., a Television News Production Certificate from New York University in Manhattan, N.Y., and a B.A. in Speech Pathology and Audiology from Lehman College in the Bronx, N.Y.

Furthermore, Lisa has been a mentor for Pen Americas Prison Writing Program, which helps prisoners reach their literary potential, promotes healing and rehabilitation.

Finally, some of her poems and have been published by and can be seen or purchased at Madness Muse Press Destigmatized Anthology which can be purchased at Amazon.com, http://www.moonmagazine.org., Civilized Beasts Vol. III at Weasel Press.com, http://www.praxismagonline.com, www.youblisher.com/pdf/884760, Obsidian III, Journal of Poetry Therapy, Footsteps, AIM, Left Jab, Poetry Motel, poemhunter.com, Peaceful Poetry to Love Your Societal Consciousness, and elsewhere.

Her published articles are:
1. Rhodes, L. (2011). Poetry writing as a healing method in coping with a special needs child: A narrative perspective. Journal of Poetry Therapy: The Interdisciplinary Journal of Practice, Theory, Research and Education, V 24, n 2 p.117-125 Sum
2. Rhodes, L. (2002). Poetry and a prison writing program: A mentor's narrative report. Journal of Poetry Therapy, v15 n3 p163-68 Spr

www.ingramcontent.com/pod-product-compliance
Lightning Source LLC
LaVergne TN
LVHW040118080426
835507LV00041B/1755